Kansas City Metropolitan

Verse

Compiled By
Missi Rasmussen

Volume 1 – 2007

Kansas City Metropolitan Verse – Volume 1

ISBN 978-1-4303-2080-7

www.lulu.com ID: 854085

Inspiration and compilation: Missi Rasmussen

Cover Art and Editing: Brenda Conley

Tech Wrangler: Ralph Acosta

Acknowledgements

The Kansas City Chapter of the Missouri Poetry Society would like to thank the following for their support in helping our organization grow stronger:

Pat Berge, Director of WriterHouse, where we hold our bi-weekly meetings, for providing space for our poems to spread out. Without WriterHouse, we would still be crouching around the coffee table in someone's cramped living room.

Margaret Clark and the Kansas City Public Library, for including us in so many National Poetry Month activities, and for giving us the opportunity to provide our services to touring poets involved with the Branching Out program in 2005.

Will Leathem, The Writers Place, and Prospero's Books in Kansas City, for enthusiastic exposure.

Michael Wells for all the hard work you do for the chapter, including formatting and maintaining the blog, www.kcmopoets.blogspot.com and for your coverage on www.stickpoetsuperhero.blogspot.com.

Ralph Acosta for being *the audience*, proofreading, attending readings, being pulled onto the stage to read, and especially for your technical support.

Brenda Conley, chapter secretary and editor, who worked extremely hard to put together this volume. How many copies of the "finished" anthology did you send for a "final" look? The amount of time and attention you have given this anthology has been phenomenal.

Dedication

Thank you to all our families: husbands, wives, boyfriends, girlfriends, sons, and daughters who we all leave when we go to "those poetry meetings" every other Tuesday. The amount of support and consideration from our families is overwhelming. This book is dedicated to each of you.

If you would like more information about

Kansas City Metropolitan Verse

or any chapter of the Missouri Poetry Society,

please visit www.nfsps.org.

TABLE OF CONTENTS

Scot Isom

Don Fessler

Bernita Pettit

Missi Rasmussen

Introduction

Kansas City Metropolitan Verse, the Kansas City Chapter of the Missouri Poetry Society, is a diverse group of poetry writers, readers, and teachers whose main objective is to help support the promotion of poetry in the Kansas City community. Founded in January, 2005, Kansas City Metropolitan Verse has encouraged the appreciation of poetry by donating poetry books to various organizations, fostering young poets in area schools, providing receptions for touring poets, and hosting poetry reading and writing events.

We hope you will enjoy this collection of poetry written and compiled by the chapter's members. We hope that not only does this book find its place on your poetry bookshelf, but that poetry itself finds its place in your life.

Missi Rasmussen
Chapter President
Kansas City Metropolitan Verse
May, 2007

REBECCA STALLARD

The Importance of Being Poe

Once upon a marvelous day, as I was bound about my way,
An extraordinary dream passed across the vision of my eye.
Once inside this inclination, overwhelmed with exhortation,
I felt as if this observation spoke the truth and would not lie.
I vow to you this honestly. I pledge it true least I should die,
This I swear not knowing why.

I saw a man, I viewed his mind. His words were dark yet he was kind.
A passion flowed inside his truthful and implicit human sigh.
I almost fought this apparition, fearing it hallucination.
Then I had a revelation. Knowing this, I said good-bye.
I said farewell unto my fear of this vaporous man so nigh.
Yet again, not knowing why.

I lingered closer, closer still. Somewhere beyond my strongest will,
I found the strength to lend my ear and hear the suffering of his cry.
I departed not the situation, but felt a sense of obligation
To fairly seek examination, and understand, as only I
Could comprehend this valiant man and his intrepid mortal sigh.
He then looked unto the sky.

I spoke "hello" unto this ghost, who in return proposed a toast.
But I sensed a sorrow coming from the tone of his reply.
I looked at him with reservation, and with no further hesitation,
(For I knew my destination) I said to him, "Please tell me why.
Why have you chosen for this task a humble woman such as I?"
Still he looked unto the sky.

I spoke these words, "Please look at me. A famous man I want to see."
But in his answer rang a truth, "*Do not you see, no fame have I?*
I sit alone in contemplation and ponder why such indignation
has put me in a situation where I am left alone to die.

Listen well unto my words, I speak the truth, I will not lie
I have chosen now to die--

My life will soon be ending. My countenance requires tending.
I must therefore seek the manner as to implore my last good-bye.
I have chosen isolation for this toxic situation.
I'll ignore humiliation as through the old man's blinded eye
And sequester one last triumph before ascension to the sky."
Once again I wondered why…

Why such a man, just at his peak, would think of life as now so bleak,
And yearn for one last living breath to conquer now his last reply.
I then yelled with much frustration, "Renounce your great imagination!
I hope a stench of condensation stays with you until you die."
A puzzled look then stained this man, and he alone began to cry.
Then he breathed a heavy sigh.

The words I spoke I did regret, but all too soon, he did forget.
A Raven perched upon a post and caught the gleaming of our eye.
"Ah!" He said, *"Communication from the bird of information.*
It's a sign of confrontation; the days of yore are in his cry.
Can you hear the echo of Lenore croaking deep within his cry?
It speaks of the days gone by."

He looked abreast while leaning, provoking thoughts that had new meaning.
Then he spoke unto the Raven sitting on the post near by.
"I implore your true intention! Speak, thou bird of ebony dissention
And give your credit of invention to the poet, mainly I.
I say swear upon your blackened crest, give true merit, don't be shy,
To the poet, mainly I."

I heard the fowl from the days of yore croak the phrase of "Nevermore."
And after setting wings to fly, took ascension to the sky.
Edgar fought a deep depression for on his face a bare expression
Took the place of his profession. No longer would his thoughts comply
To a simple sound or written phrase. No more words — far or nigh.
"None," he said, "No more have I."

My heart was filled with passion to view a man in such a fashion,
And to ponder now his reasoning for such a laden measure – Why?
Why such a vast imagination would linger now in meditation,
Searching for a situation to end a melancholy sigh.
"If you think you've been forgotten, you're simply incorrect," said I.
"Please, for me, get up and try."

I saw the look upon his face and knew it wasn't now my place,
To reason to a broken heart whose shattered dreams would soon comply
To the final confrontation inside his futile obligation.
And with no further explanation, I understood the reason why,
Why now this providence in time was to be seen by my own eye!
Then I breathed a heavy sigh.

The reason for this flash of light was so that others one day might
Comprehend the cause of the mysterious way this man did die.
It seems his inspiration had a mistaken reputation,
And no appreciation had been revealed by one human eye.
He then spoke as would a friend unto the woman such as I.
"On your heart you must rely….

I thank you for your faith and trust, but now you know I simply must
Unearth the path which leads unto my sweet Virginia in the sky."
With a hint of reservation, he waved me on,—*"Imagination,*
Creative innovation, is the key to a poem. 'Trust!' 'Rely!'—
Now on about your merry way to ponder on these words from I."
And he waved to me good-bye.

My desire was then to stay, but I took the path of my own way,
And I never shall forget the presence of that vision in my eye.
I had a fresh appreciation from the man of inspiration.
This gave me new foundation to know his words would now comply
To all the words that would be written by the woman such as I.
I then looked unto the sky.

I saw his spirit flowing, where it went I'm left not knowing,
But I'm sure it lingers close for my mind is such I can't deny
The lack of concentration it takes for my imagination
To create the duplication of discerning thoughts that only I
Would see. For I have seen the reason why this famous man did die.
This I swear, I do not lie

Waves Against The 'C'

The children are crying, the reason, they said,
"Our mother is gone, our mother is dead.
She drowned in the 'C,' it took her away,
Now we've nowhere to go, and nowhere to play."

The children are trying to cope with their fear,
"Why did mom have to go, who will care for us here?"

"She's not really gone," said the young one believing,
In hopes that the others would soon stop their grieving.
"Mom wouldn't go and leave us alone,
She knows we can't cope with the world on our own."

The children are lying so they don't have to face
The cruel realization of death and its place.

Then one of the children, who was oldest—and wise,
Said, "The world doesn't stop when somebody dies;
No matter how much we love her and want her to be,
She's better off now where her spirit is free."

Now, the children are grown, but they feel incomplete,
For they lost in their life what was precious and sweet.

No one could stop their sweet mother from dying,
And inside their dear hearts, the children, are still crying.

The Tears of Hamlet

Hamlet was crying, the reason, he said, "My father is gone, my father is dead. He slept in the garden, he died where he lay, Now I've nowhere to go and nowhere to play."

Hamlet was trying to cope with his fear. "Why did dad have to go, who will care for me here?"
"He's not really gone," said his best friend Horatio, "He lives in a spirit, He's a ghost don't you know."

The ghost said to Hamlet, "You won't be alone, I give you a clue to reflect on your own: Claudius is lying so he won't have to face what will come of his life if he's put in his place— My once faithful brother did poison my ear, now he sleeps with my wife and he drinks the king's beer."

Hamlet, forlorn at the rumor he heard, said, "Father this news sounds rather absurd. But I vow to you now, a vengeance I swear, I'll catch my dear uncle and become the true heir."

The spirit told Hamlet, "To your mother be true, though she did break my heart, she still doth love you."

Hamlet was puzzled! He stood and he thought. Hamlet then spoke of what is and what's not: "The question at hand: Is death not to be, Shall we slumber and sleep, or to die shall we? And if we die and sleep, 'What dreams may come?' I'm rather dismayed at the future of some. And why does it seem that everyone's lying? Why all of these tears? Why still am I crying?"

Hamlet set out on a tedious quest, but ran into spies who gave him a test. An acquaintance named Rose, another one Guild, made Hamlet to speak and caused him to yield. "Tell me my peers, whom were you sent for? Why come you this day to the place Elsinore?"

His peers did reply, "'Twas our own inclination. To visit you Lord, no other occasion."
Hamlet sensed Claudius behind this foul lie. "I will set up a trap and shall see who doth cry. I'll call for a play, observe the King's looks, and if he is guilty, I'll see if he books."

Hamlet conversed with his true love, Ophelia. He said, "Are you honest?" Ophelia said, "Duh! Why question my fairness, why question my vow? I say, 'woe is me,' why question me now?"

But Hamlet fed up with his girlfriend of woe, said, "Get ye my love; to a nunnery GO!"
Hamlet complained of his woman so fickle. (And then found himself in a rather tight pickle). He had a clear chance to stab the false king, but Hamlet delayed, this came as a sting. "If I kill him now, in heaven he stays, his soul shall be worthy, for Claudius prays."

Meanwhile Polonius, with Gertrude (in reign) hid near the curtain to spy for his gain.
In entered Hamlet. He yelled at his Ma: "Disloyal were you! I blame you for Pa! My father, God rest, has been much offended. The fault is on you for his life to have ended."

Gertrude in fear, cried out, "Help! Help! Ho!" And Hamlet with sword, to the curtain did go.

Hamlet said, "Fool! His blood does now stain;" and Polonius (dad of Ophelia) was slain.

Gertrude proclaimed, "Oh, what have I done, to bring out the wrath of Hamlet, my son?"
Hamlet replied, "Oh Ma, you've been blind. The words that I speak must be 'cruel to be kind.'"

Now shifting to song, Ophelia did sing, "Hamlet refuses to give me a ring.-
I once was a maid, and Hamlet did take, my soul I now drown. My own life forsake."

Then back at the castle in Denmark of Yore,
'A Method of Madness' was what was in store. A man named Laertes, whose sister had drowned, conveyed unto Hamlet, "You'll never be crowned."
(A scheme with the King had been prearranged), The sword fight was on, and poison exchanged.

Claudius then dropped a poisonous pearl,
Intended for Hamlet (not for his girl).

The queen took a sip of the victory wine,
"I am poisoned," said she, "My life is not mine."

Tears mixed with vengeance consumed Hamlet's force; and he killed, who do you think? Claudius, of course.

Hamlet now wailed for all that was lost, "I avenged as I swore, only life was the cost."

Laertes last words: "Please Hamlet, forgive." And, "I must inform you, you neither shall live.- Swords tipped in toxins now run through our veins, not much we can do, but die with our pains."

Hamlet then knew his life would be ending, no cure for his blood, no future ascending. "Let Fortinbras' son take over the throne… Name Horatio, 'Dane.' Now I die as I moan."

Then no one could stop dear Hamlet from crying;
For the great prince himself, Hamlet, was now dying.

BRENDA CONLEY

Ma

Pulled back from her face
twisted up in a bun,
her hair,
when loosened,
allowed to fall,
I remember it
nearly reached the floor
from the chair she sat in
as I brushed
with four year old skill and
reveled in the beauty
as nature changed it
from silver at the crown
to tips of dark, dark brown.

Conversation with Chloe, age 4

Grandma, when I'm a big girl,
like Rachel,
and you call me on the phone,
I'll come to where you are.
And I'll bring my dog
so he can stay with you
while I go to school.
I'll have a car,
like Rachel's car.
and a dog
to stay with you,
because
my real mom doesn't like dogs
but you do
and I do.

My House is Quiet

My house is quiet.
For the first time in my life
I live alone.
I'm not sure whether to like it or not.
Then I see people trying
to keep their dog under control,
their teenager under control,
their laundry under control,
I say thank heaven for quiet.
Sometimes I am lonesome,
living alone, but
still have an old Siamese cat to pet me.
Doesn't greet me at the door
like the dogs did, though.
She likes to curl up on my lap
while I drink my coffee.
She bumps the cup to get my attention
and I give thanks for inconvenience.

My Grandson the Musician

I awoke to the sound of a fly
as he plucked a string of my guitar.
It stood leaned against the wall
of my room.
I reached for it, began to play
before my feet touched the floor.

If I Could Drink a Beer With Anyone

If I could drink a beer with anyone
I'd drink it with my brother.
Him, the beast from a paper case
Me, a stout from a frosted glass
We'd speak fondly of our mother.

I'd give him the news
Hope he doesn't forget
to peel the grapes,
the seed is planted,
your boy is soon to be a father.

He'd ask about the dogs.
We'd even talk about my job.
Conversation would flow,
then slow.

I'd drag it on, though,
As long as I could.
As long as I could
And I'd drink a beer with my brother.

Dreamer

Sweet pastry circle
pinched 'tween thumb and pointer,
she'd drifted off to Nappie's house,
touched fingers to her mouth,
then startled awake to realize
she was only dreaming.

Origin, History

Silence broken by the sound
of a whirring sewing machine.
Silence of no children, no TV.
Silence of a sleeping puppy.
The photographer comes tonight
Green and white stripes must
be applied to the hemline by 5:30

Straight pins contained
in a swatch of cloth.
Pincushion stayed behind
with my middle child, my sewing child.
The only one interested in
sharing my machine for her own pleasure,
also shares my supplies:
needles and thread, shears, measuring tape and
handmade crocheted pincushion.

Decades ago variegated pastel threads
became a hand-sized spring bonnet.
Woven blue ribbon, now faded,
encircles the fiber filled crown.
Brim, once stiff with starch, has
softened by use and years

My mother bought the treasure
at a thrift store on Quality Hill.
Gave it to me to use through junior high Home EC,
then to make my graduation dress,
(yellow, fully lined, challenge for a teen)
at twenty, became my wedding dress.
Used while making little dresses for my babies,
now simple, child-sized quilts for my grandchildren

I've decided to call my daughter today
at her job and tell her about it,
how important it is to me.
Remind her of its origin, its history
and that I would like for her to have it.

The Huckster

I would be willing to bet it was red.
Piled high.
A scale hung from a shaft
attached to the corner of the bed.

As he stopped to vend his wares
my dad stood
on the curb
or on the brick street's edge.

I know they talked.
Know not what they said.
They were men.
I was a child.

The huckster carved a wedge
from the watermelon
for approval, his guarantee.

The fruit was fresh.
The vegetables crisp.
The gift he gave my baby brother,
Yellow.

George and Mattie

Never seem to find it
as quickly as I'd like to.
Bronze Iris, dark patina
alongside a bench placed
for another family.
George and Mattie side by side
over half a century married
lie for eternity together.

She was sixteen years old,
her first date, maybe.
He was twenty seven,
had served his country in the army,
been away and now was home.
He saw her across the lawn
beside the lakeshore
at a picnic with her sisters
and their boyfriends.
I'm sure of one thing-
he fell in love.

They rowed a canoe, kissed,
then they were married.
That's how she told the story.
Simple, their life together.
Her family, their children
he left his sisters and his brothers
to join hers.

AMY LEIGH

The Listener

For Ramona

A Word.
Only One.
The First One
will one day
escape those virgin lips.

No guidance.
Only instinct.
Only nature.

The Word itself
does not matter.
It is Time.

Time to study the
rise and fall of
my voice.
Father's voice.
The voices of the world
she never chose to enter.

The silent listener
of definite formed syllables
she will one day inherit
as her native tongue.

Every day,
I tell her my stories.
Some with meaning,
some without,
so she may one day
tell her own.

A Young Woman with Father

My father sat beside me
at a bar and grill in good ole' Tennessee.
The scent of steak sauce, onions and oil
lingered in the air.
The strong stench of Jack Daniels made my stomach
curl up in a ball.

I leaned up against the wooden bar,
my finger outlining initials
that had been engraved
in the wood from past lives.

I sipped my glass of wine and took a drag
off a stogy.
I watched my father, who sat next to me.
He spoke, his voice deep and dry:

If only there was more time,
If only you did not leave tomorrow,
We would go back there…back to the country.

My scars bled and the colors of the country
flashed before me.
I could see it if I closed my eyes,
I could see in a vacant stare.

It was the spring of '85,
dissolving and evolving here.
My papa went into the house with
a double barrel shotgun
on a cattle ranch in back woods Tennessee.

The sun smiled in the cloudless blue sky.
The grandchildren played in
the fields and by the streams.
Bees buzzed in the air and
the scent of clean wet grass and
manure lingered like dew on our skin.

Papa lay in his bed,
shoved the cold steel metal into his mouth
and Click-
pulled the trigger.
The shot rang out into the day.
Silence Fell.

A child, I wanted to laugh
at the ringing in my ears,
thinking it the fourth of July.
Though a child I was,
I sensed the fear and anguish
in my father's eyes.

My mother swept me into her arms,
carrying me away from
the white house with the black shutters.
My eyes fixed on my father as the earth moved
farther and farther away from him.

My father, the solider that stood
strong and proud,
crying, in the midst of his own battlefield.
My father sat lost in a vacant stare
haunted by the reality of the silent years.

Life Habitual

In the last months,
nothing is enough.
Everything has been done.
The book has reached its
climax.

Life has flat-lined.
You are King Solomon
in a Kansas City suburb.

Those closest to you
are closer than ever to you
yet they do not even occupy your
space, your time.

Welcome to the Utopian jail cell.
You can have everything,
yet nothing is what you find.

Psychiatry almost seems a
promising course of action.
Such a hideous thought,

to pay someone to hear
your thoughts,
to pay someone for the
company of the world.

With not word to offer,
only the dumb eyes
and planned voice.

While you lay back
and make a witness
for your vanished dreams

Relativity

Silence. Silence.
The sun strains
through a slit in a leaf.
A never-ending horizon
stretches across the great expanse.

The mountain looms in the distance.
It is huge and I am small.
It is all relative.
Einstein was a poet scientist.

I can close one eye
and place my hand on it - the mountain
without walking a step
If you ask the worms
they will say I am already on it

with my giant's feet
and limbs.
Why, they are the rings of Saturn
The moons fit snug,
against the edge of my thigh
praising the comets that fly.

If you ask the universe
she would say she is above it,
a sort of bleuglow hue and white too.
As a whole, nothing really looks like it.
The mountain rises and rolls with the land.
The Earth must have been full of itself
growing its insides into empty,
much like the beginning -
nothing happening and becoming everything.

A World Coming Down

Somewhere in the darkness,
there is a ray of light cast
through a broken building,
the roof caving in on itself.
.
The earth has risen to claim
the foundation,
leaving mounds of dirt.
Yet the naked boards
of the four walls still stand

holding all of what once
fit together.
The winds howl and
the wood creaks and groans
knowing how it must
come apart
.

Still Life

This room I am in
was once walked through
but never sat in.

Now, it is where I spend
most of my time.
I have become familiar
with the old brick mantle.

The blackened brick within,
is the future of fires past.
The painting above the mantle,

a real life image on canvas,
capturing the white and pink
blossoms in bloom before
the petals begin to wither.

SCOT ISOM

Cul De Sac

My thought daggers fall wasted
Well from their marks
Bruising conformity's pristine lawns
Only an irritant to manicure on Sunday morning
While suburbia's heart beats on
Immune from criticism
In cul de sac caves
Ignoring everything not of their cookie cutter world
God, church and Wal Mart pilgrimages

…And I saw The Amazing Dark Hair

Panther shadowed in burgundy flame
Her hair
Framing features flavored with fire
Oh-my-God-amazing
Candle lit contours of elegance
With hints of danger
Like thorns of the rose
Worth the pain to experience the beauty

Of mirth
Revelry
and contentment

As her smile echoes her flame
Too hot to touch
Too fine to resist

So burn and reburn
Sensate beauty and Joie de vie
Her eyes - imagination sparks
Fuel the flame

And I smile having experienced
in simplicity
Pure art

June 20, 2005

Tomorrow smiles - you smile
Today into tomorrow
Words into chapters
A life - our time together
You knew I loved you
Before I accepted what my heart was saying
You knew - always knew
We would be together

Chartreuse to crimson
The sunrise and June 20, 2005
By sunset -
I asked for your hand
For you had my heart

Ars Poetica

The poems come
In excruciating agony
As pustules half formed
Half decayed
On the page
And poem after poem is born
Deformed
Unformed
Harming all they touch
...and still I write
Hating my children

The Back of the Sock Drawer

Mateless commas on the bedspread
Useless halffunctions of whatoncewas

Lost in process
Onceunits going in
Orphans coming out

Time passes
As they take up space
And eventually
Forgotten with nopurpose

To Wake and See You Smile

To wake and see you smile
Kitten content - no worries
For the moment and horizons
In all directions - sunshine
Considering today is all that matters
And tomorrows line up as open doors
With breezes bringing Spring-scents

Giant Heart

Giant heart anticipated the big burn
Sitting subtle giving deft philosophy
In cello baritone

In sparse words Giant Heart
Specifics wisdom and smiles
In warm waves toward everyone

As conversation flows from smile
To smile he listens nodding
The comfort of friends

Giant Heart
Improved all he knew
In word caresses as brilliant as flowers
Ideas the sublime of sunset

The good doctor, the giant man
From dust to ash, opened many lives
A space we can never fill

Thanksgiving On A Dock In Olongapo

As the wood of the ammo box splinters a foot
above my head, I imagine a Filipino man
looking down a barrel through his sights,
centering on my head. Exhaling, squeezing

the trigger and then another bullet hits the ammo
box, splinters fly, poking my cheek, and my
bladder wants to empty. Ski calls on the radio,
Where are they? Where are they? I whisper.

Fuck if I know, the jungle, the jungle. I'm
pinned down. I hear them yell, we'll kill
you cocksucker, and more bullets splinter the
wood. I watch the jungle, touched by dock lights,

creating heavier darks beyond the glow. And
voices yell from the black and I peer looking for
shadows to move. Curse the light which illuminates
me in full glow. The bullets pin me for four hours.

Not once do I see a face as my squad maneuvers to flank
them in the jungle. Eventually the bullets stop, fading with
them into the shadows. Finally I stick my head up, my
uniform dotted red from where the splinters wounded my cheek
.

Only A Few Ounces…

Weighing only a few ounces,
accelerated to several hundred miles an hour.
It hits the skin, tears the sac separating

fluid and the world. - enters, shatters bone,
slowly losing speed, but driving forward
piercing through tissue, liver, lungs,

and finding the heart. Which beats
faster, faster, faster, faster
trying to rush blood and oxygen

to the wounds, but after a few
moments, beats slower, slower.
Stops.

Only a piece of lead in lifeless meat
That was once: Mother Daughter Sister Lover Friend
And another few ounces at high velocity...

Iam lsto

The ideas, the concepts
the quagmire of too many, to sort, to understand,
of opposing views, of opposition, of destruction,
as words, written and spoken, few understood, few accepted
as most fly on past, to the past, gone before I can understand them,
as channels change, and pages turn, too quickly, too gone, too gone, too gone,
I am lost.

As I sit at my computer, writing, composing, decomposing, the words of the great,
I realize how few, and how too many the greats were, and the greats aren't and
I start
confused, cfoneusued - iedas, cceonpts, hTe sntecne, as I wtrie it, bceoems cfseonud nda
lsot in oot mnay iedas form yteredeasy nad tdoay. aWtl hiWmtamn is het fehtar of dab
pertoy.

So I srot het iedas oznigarng tehm by ptirioy an

Iam lsto.

Dorothy Parker's News Item (My Take)

Dorothy Parker's sardonic quip
Offers women this subtle tip
Men seldom make passes
At girls who wear glasses.

But nearsighted ladies don't you fear
As I share a thought from me as a peer
Some shortsighted men may fail to see
The stunning allure - the beauty of she.

Wearing lenses perched for sight
Adds a dimension, a depth, a bite
A sexy side of mystery and poise
Unfathomable for men in search of toys.

As for me, with confidence I say
The women I see throughout the day
While I always check your boobs and asses
My gaze always settles on your glasses.

So ladies Dorothy Parker's advice is poor
Her words are humorous nothing more
For some men always make passes
At girls who wear glasses.

DON FESSLER

A Midnight Dark

In the cemetery of the midnight dark
Restless souls sing a dirge
Lamenting not their demise but last
Offerings of hope

Forever wondering and lost in maybes and could have been
Souls of the damned twist and turn
Their being poured on burning coals
They no longer willing nor able to repent of past sin.

What is and will be is eternally recorded
And non-negotiable
Past, present, future only found
In the permanent unchangeable present tense

Neither sunrays nor starbeams can guide their travels once more
From the marble forest of lost beings
All hope has been banished
Nor does love pay a visit

Judgment's steel curtain lowers and seals out even a morsel
Of remorse of conscience
The stench of un-repented past sins fills the nostrils
With revulsion and self-loathing…eternally
With no hope, trust, nor love
Banished to the company of the Prince of Darkness
The disciples of death
They shall be permanently poured into non-forgiving cement

Throw no prayer toward these banished lost souls
For all compassion is melted in Hades
And Mercy is a stranger without a companion
Lost in a foreign land

All ye who fall here put all fantasy of relief from pain behind you
Flames lick the souls, destroying
Not even a drop of water is there to refresh their parched tongues
The flames of Hell are stoked by anger

Special tortures are fashioned
Custom made for each damned soul in pits of fire with no respite
Oh torture so vast their pain that can never be relieved
The foremost of torture, most dreaded,
Is permanent banishment from the entrance door of God Almighty

Those sins that were their delight at one time are now their eternal agony
Oh Pilgrim, kneel in firm mercy prayer that souls will not taste Hell
Be warned, no one in anger say, "Go to Hell"
It will in guilt shadow their own soul

Remember that the kiss of honey
Is better than the stench of sulfur

Love

Love who is not loved.
It is I who loves the unloved
When I reach out to touch
It is love that gathers the fruit.
When fear fogs the way,
Anxiety runs amuck, it is you, beloved,
That smoothes the path to peace.
When the soul is famished for holy desires
Loves not for gain, nor gold, nor even health,
But loves only for love,
Then all becomes Heaven bound.

When Night's Shade is Drawn

When daylight shatters the dawning new day
When night's shade is withdrawn
The rising sun makes its début

Then like flames kindling for a new day
Be blessed, immersed in the freshness
Of the meadow

Holy day begin, I sing my song
To the source of all maternal love
Mother Most Holy

Blessed mother of God
I humbly request that like the morn,
Fresh cover me with your holy veil

In all my vain and humble efforts
On the portal of this day listen
Tenderly to my petition

When I struggle in vain and am torn asunder
Let be a song to thee in hope
Wherever I chance to be, let it be
Under the shadow of the Immaculate Heart

Oh, Mother of God, in all my efforts
Hopes, struggles, dreams may they be
According to my dearest Mother, copied

Let me own not things that melt
Under the midday sun like dripping wax
Under the shelter of the maternal fiat, may I echo
In her heart and in my Holy Mother's footsteps

Bless me most Holy Mother as
Your own adopted son- now and forever
In gratitude I offer up these inadequate words
To my beloved most Holy Mother

Tell Me Hon

The candles on our 50th wedding anniversary cake
have melted down, the guests have all gone.
Tell me, Hon, Do you still love me
or has the wax of our love melted away?
Do you remember way back when,
our love was once fresh and had legs?
Now it is not always present, but
do you remember when our love was here to stay?
Did time, place, and hurt leave us wounded?
Leave us together, alone?
Do we stand alone, lying in bed
strangers, side by side?
Tell me, Hon, do you still love me
or are we driftwood on different sandy shores?
When we talk, do our words fly past one another
at the speed of light?
We once shared the same love song
now our music is a separate anthem sung out of tune.
Time and distance have come and gone.
Can we gather sea shells on ocean's shore once more?
Tell me, Hon, do you still love me
or have our tears dried up,
no longer run down our wrinkled cheeks?
Kiss me once more, if nothing else,
for old time's sake and remembrance.
Tell me, Hon, do you still love me?

Number 149 Bus

On rubber wings the Taipei to Ti Chung
Number 149 bus rambles due south.
On the right hand side, she takes a seat

On Saturday we make this encore
In anticipated romance
This dance of love

Fly south to me my love
As I hide this weekend
In the folds of my dreams

South China breezes gently accompany
Ti Ti past fragrant aromas
Of beechnut farms, past rice farmers

Knee deep in green water
Leading carabao planting this years crop

Past ever ripe green sugarcane fields
Pregnant with sweet syrup
Soft South Sea breezes bring these

Aromas to the back roads of my mind
Stand still frosty mind
And remember

Amore' amore'

The drum beat of the early moonshine
Rains a chorus on the tin roof of
The bus station as I wait

Remember a drab room in the Fortuna Hotel
One block from the bus station
Grapes no one could eat on the papered walls

In my stuffy room
Fluorescent lights snap on
Play their patterns on the wall

Can one night of love
Drive away
Six nights of alone

Amore' amore'

Ti Ti's scent lifts like the aroma
Of the South China Sea
Lifts from the pillow as I lay alone

The lazy turning ceiling fan
Stirs her perfume back and forth
Like mountain scent breezes.

She promenades on my bedroom ceiling
Each night where words have no meaning
For they are mere words

Amore' Amore'

On the crowded streets below
People make music under my window
Night and day

Street vendors hustle
Crying out their value
To souls pretending no interest

Food carts push out onto the crowded sidewalk
The bus rolls past the vendors selling sweet rice
To taste for Ten NT

Let summer shadows lengthen
Cover gray dwellings
To wait for night time breezes

Though the life of the city groans
Declares life is
Here and present

Amore' Amore'

The lonely call of the tin whistle
Haunts all to its blind mans alert

To loosen the tired bones and muscles
For one hundred Fifty NT
On a downtown conveyor

Two illegal Filipino boys strum their guitars
And sing *Sad movies always make me cry*
Lovers hold hands
Keep a sharp eye out for momma's glare

Only feeds my lonesome self
To singing along
On street's corner

Room service put through the usual call
To Ti Ti in Taipei
And please don't listen in.

Hi Sweetheart
Wrap things up on Saturday
And send yourself south

Why, do you miss me?
I am famished for you
Say yes!

So goes our game of charades
Always leading to
Yes

Amore' amore'

There she rolls in a shower of mud
Scattering stones and pebbles
The number 149 bus

From Taipei to Tai Chung
Has presented itself
No need to remind you friends

I have in days past
Been well loved

Amore' Amore'

BERNITA PETTIT

Scent of Rain

darkness was upon us
as I parked the VW near the waters edge
and stepped out on the damp gravel-bed.
all three followed, as expected
their small hands groping
security found in the form of a shirt-tail
my fears heightening
as I listen to their curious chatter.
peering into the dark
I moved toward the upper-bank
and started climbing
ready for the new challenge.
they followed closely
questioning unfamiliar sounds
young imaginations
magnified by the dark.
soon the sound of a crackling fire
its flames painting an orange glow
on their young faces
with amber sparks leaping about
and more assuring answers
to their wonders of the night.
the burning drift-wood
slowly turned into
a pile of smoldering gray ashes.
wrapped in blankets near the fire
their eyelids grew heavy
and they drifted into a slumberous state.
with my fears slowly diminishing
I lay gazing at the stars
sprayed across the sky like specks of silver paint
while listening to the roar of the water
spilling over the dam
into the calm, quiet flow of the Osage.
a flicker of light on the western horizon
I felt a gentle midnight breeze
laced with the scent of rain.

A Promise

Shaky fingers run thru
Over-processed
Bleached-blonde hair.
She's lost her comb.

With the palm of her hand
She presses at the wrinkles
Nervously adjusting the front
Of her faded t-shirt.

She glances around
Then shrugs,
No worse than the others

The appointment's at three.
It's five till.
The clock ticks
And she waits.

She wants to leave,
But remembers a promise.
So she stays
And waits.

Her name is called.
She walks across the room
Pausing at the door.
The washed-out logo
On the back of her t-shirt reveals
Summer Jam-1974.
She steps inside
And closes the door.

Blanket of Green

Watching him quietly prepare
For his Saturday morning chore,
I asked if I could help
He said no.

Lifting the mower from the shed
He walks across the yard
Pulling the mower behind
Heading for his starting point.

The first row was always cut
Along the edge of the wire fence
Then row after row he walked
The length of the yard, back and forth.

With a tight grip on the handle
He pushed the old mower
Through the thick summer grass
Each row slightly overlapping.

Rotating mower blades,
Recently honed,
Trimmed beneath the heavy peonies
Around thick iris beds.

Then, the clip, clip, clipping sound
As he pushed the mower closely
Where I sat under the
Fruitless, old cherry tree

Tossing in the air, freshly cut grass
Damp with the early morning dew
A blanket of green,
Falling across my bare legs.

Bobby

It isn't the music.
It isn't the voice.
It's all in the lyrics
Words written by choice.

He started with folk
And strummed with the best
Then followed his instincts
Moved on with great zest.

He played Folk-Rock
And electric guitar.
Moved Country and Blues
And became a big star.

He sang about the times
And what he believed.
He answered their questions
With slight tongue-in-cheek.

I protest with the music
That's what I do.
It's all in the lyrics
My way of talking to you.

He traveled the globe
Like a Rolling Stone
From city to country
But longing for home…

He wrote the great music
He signed with the labels
Then the bike took a toss
It was 8 years till he was stable.

The times, they are a-changing,
he wrote, but he is still
The Essential
Bob Dylan

Teddy

Spiraling thru the air,
Watching in anticipation
Its destination left un-said
Needn't alter the imagination.

The ball's been passed
And well received.
Though we all knew he was ready.
'Cause he's the team's star player,
A running back named Teddy.

A move to the left
Then back to the right
To find that open hole.
A swift move forward now
Will put him near the goal.

Now comes the play he's waited for
Like so many times before.
Worn cleats step over the goal-line
To tally up the score.

Well, seasons come and seasons go,
And many games are won.
But now it's MVP time
For my daughter's only son.

The Door

Vintage
Rustic finish
Ajar
On hinge
Screws protruding
Broken latch
Jammed
Skeleton key
Smell of age
What lies beyond
This massive, old
Solid door?

JD SMITH

Desert Fireplace

Fiery heat
Glassy lake reflecting
The soft glow of
Dancing shadows

Warm, artful colors
Red, orange, yellow, white
The crackle of the squishy
Sandy cushion beneath
The sunset of Nature's hearth

Dream Images

Vivid upon awakening
Fade quickly
Disappear completely
Leaving an uneasy sense of loss
But of what,
I cannot say

My Life

Making...
Beds, bread, meals, to-do-lists

Making...
Decisions, plans, promises, mistakes

Making...
MY WAY in this life
Seconds, minutes, hours
Days, weeks, months

Year after Year
Boundless realm of possibilities

Spring's Flags

Go out into my garden

Inhale that sweetest of smells,
Deepest of colors,
Flashiest of ruffled skirts

A rainbow of IRIS
Enjoy!
For they will be gone too soon
As will Spring

Forgotten

Three rotten brown bananas
Forgotten entirely
Lazing in the sun, the dark, the weather

Dry,
Stiff outer hide,
Soft, mushy insides

No one has touched you
Since Aunt Lida
Placed you on the porch rail
Weeks ago to ripen for
Forgotten banana bread

Flavorful Colors of Fall

Plum, persimmon, burgundy
Mustard, blueberry, cider
Dusty sage, caramel, nutmeg

Oatmeal, coffee, chocolate
Cinnamon apple, pumpkin, cranberry
Raisin, avocado, raspberry

Yummy, yummy colors,
Fall colors, good enough to eat!

Today's Single Mothers

How she does it, I can't say…
Works forty plus hours per week
Shops, washes clothes, cooks, and cleans
Councils, corrects and comforts
Watches, teaches, analyzes,
Loves and cares
Today's single Moms
Do it all

But…

When the children grow up,
The absent father
Emerges
The Hero

Acadia in Autumn

Endless vistas
Ancient bedrock, gouged-out valleys
Mountains, ground down
Rain-fed cascades, deep lakes, rocky coves
Water washed shores of unpredictable ocean

Carriage roads, hiking trails
Horses, bicycles, pedestrians

Painted foliage, birch and sedge
Wild blueberry bushes
Windswept granite boulders and moss covered rocks

Captivating sunrises and sunsets
Bright days and cool nights
Scarlet prominence of maple's flare
The pyrotechnic display of aurora colored night skies

Mount Dessert Island
Bar Harbor and Jordan Pond
Sand Dollar Beach and Cadillac Mountain
Thunder Hole
Come enjoy this peaceful respite

TERRY WEIDE

Time to Be Leaving

It's time to be leaving,
I should have left a year ago,
But felt constrained to stay.
Now the constraint is gone,
The debt of life and karma has
    been paid.
The things I need to do to learn
and grow are far from here;
I avoid taking new jobs,
Making new friends,
Avoid the entanglements that
    bind one to a place,
Avoid entering relationships it
    would hurt to break.
Take a pair of psychic scissors,
Snip the strings of attachment,
Free both the past and myself.
Good-bye to Kansas City,
A month or two more and then
It's time to go.

in response to dylan thomas, july 4 – 5, 2002

Go Bravely Into That New Horizon

Go bravely into that new horizon,
Young age laughs at the dawning of the day;
Sing, sing, the rising of the sun.

New men at their start know the light is strung,
And because their words have conjured magic they
Go bravely into that new horizon.

Transcendent men, the first flow by, lightly sung
Their deeds are dancing on the scrolls of fate,
Sing, sing, the rising of the sun.

Enlightened men, who embrace and love orisons,
And who realize their potential is awake,
Go bravely into that new horizon.

Happy men, near life, who see with psychic vision,
Celestial eyes that glow like auras and do not look away,
Sing, sing, the rising of the sun.

And you, my son, there in the heavenly prism,
Save me, baptize me, with your strong blood, I pray.
Go bravely into that new horizon,
Sing, sing, the rising of the sun.

The Quick Brown Fox

The quick brown fox,
Jumps over the lazy dogs.
He leads them through a
Valley of silver pines
That shiver in the wind.
He skips across fields of
Green wheat and creeks of ice.
The barks from the pack fade.
Slowing, he lets the dogs
Close,
Then grins back--
Sticking his tongue out.
Circling them through
Brown grass and stick tights,
He comes from behind and
Does it again.
The quick brown fox
Jumps over the lazy dogs.

One Last Mystical Trip

It's been a long time since I've been to this place.
The wind surrounds it like an ocean, through which I
must swim/strive/struggle.
Leaves hiss at my approach as I attain the shore and reach
that center which is everywhere.
I hold the sun, cupped, in my hands, and the moon in my hair.
My back is against the tree, Yagdrassil, and I draw power
from it, merge with it—
Roots deep in the mysteries of the Earth,
Stars drifting through the branches,
Whispering their secrets,
As fish impart their wisdom only to the reef.
Or the Leviathan, or each other.
And I become part of all things and they of me—
I am ghostly nebulae and moonlit spiderwebs,
I am the black crow and the coyote,
I am chalk-white tombstones
In late afternoon graveyards,
To whom the dead murmur their stories
Like forgotten springs of the past.
And I am the snow, and I am the shadow,
And I am the silence in the air.
It's been a long time since I've been here.
It's good to be home again.

MICHAEL A. WELLS

Sport Utility Poem

Let me shove this in your face
Guzzle up words in excess
Burn high octane adjectives
Belch superlatives your way
My verbs are bigger than yours
Because that is how I want them
Need has nothing to do with it
I could compact or subcompact
But why, when I can take my poem
Where I want- through the fucking mud
Off the page and around couplets and haikus
Into places your creampuff iambic pentameter can't go
And I'll leave you in my oxymoronic dust
Passing everything on the road
Except a dictionary- cause a guy's gotta refuel
And I don't mind that- economy is not my thing
There's an endless supply of words
So I charge ahead with my bumper
Raised high as my ego- flipping off orthodoxy

Sport Utility Poem first appeared in *Rockhurst Annual Arts Review.*

Making the Most of It

Sorting out the allegory,
Dividing up the spoils
To which we are entitled
According to some archaic law
Of our own.

These times are not the norm
And we can't quite recall normalcy
Aside from the time the catfish jumped
A good three feet above the water,
The summer the moon froze in full mode
For two straight months.

I remember old folks telling of strange sightings
In the northern sky, and they claim the winter was harsh
That year and the women all spoke in language
That would have mortified their own sensibilities
Any other time.

It seems we all adjust to changes sooner or later.
The wind is always shifting and desires are nothing more
Than wants- not needs.

All of us are looking for chances
At one time or another.
Opportunity comes and goes,
But mostly it just hangs out
In Jackson Hole.

Making the Most of It first appeared in *The Boston Literary Magazine*

A Zen Experience

So I thought I'd turn on some Reality
Television and there was a Buddha
dude with a circle of followers
setting cross-legged around him
while he spoke the truth about peace
and aviation. I liked what he said
about flight, "You can do it." and that was good
since I needed to get to Naples very quickly.
I also liked that he was ok with discount airlines
and that he recommended several personally.
I mean a tip from Buddha trumps *Consumers*
Report any day. When he was finished speaking
he gave each a chapbook of poems he had
personally written. It was not his first, he is
quite accomplished as a poet. He prefers free
verse and I think it has something to do with
his vow of poverty but I'm not sure. He would
take naught for his chapbook, asking only
that people circulate them to the masses
when finished reading them, by leaving them
in some conspicuous place at a Kinko's or
Krispy Kreme. I though this was innovative
evangelization. It must say something about
his concern for carb cravers and butt-tired students
burning candles to the god of last minute effort
on projects due yesterday. The show ended
with no preview of next week's episode.
A rerun I thought. Still, it would be new
to me as I had not seen any other episodes.
The program was sponsored by the word
breathe and the letters O, U, and T. I took
a deep breath, held it a moment and exhaled.
Then I called a discount airline to book my flight
and they asked me how I chose them. I told them
I was referred by a Buddha dude. They gave me
a 15% discount immediately and bumped me
to first class. I guess it really is not what you know
but who you know in and out of this world.

Tiananmen Mother
for Zhao Ziyang

The Beijing breeze whispers
mournful strophes.
Tears like the mountain rains
follow slopes

to tributaries until they become one
with the rippling waters of the Yangtze.

I am a Tiananmen mother.
My eyes have swelled
with this sadness before.
The wetness follows a path
well rehearsed.
My nights are immense.
I am but a lone bare branch
in a cold, dark world.

They replicate
that June night
etched in my soul
over and over.

My son stood
in the Square
armed only
with a vision
and they came-
The People's Army.

My son stood
in Tiananmen Square,
amid a sea of other
sons and daughters
and they came-

armored tanks
clanking along the streets into Tiananmen
driven by fear, ordered by paranoia.

Our sons and daughters
toppled to the earth
at their hands.
Crimson crawling into every crevice
Of these ancient Chinese streets
A stain still upon us today.

I cannot count the nights
I've wept for my son since.
Today, I weep for another.

There is no official news
but the Beijing breeze whispers again.
This time for the death of the old man.
There are guards of fear
stationed outside my door.
The lump in my throat is big,
I cannot begin to swallow,
that is how I know the truth.

Guilt always gnawing at my heart.
I could not help my son that June night.
Again as I am helpless.

I want to pay my respects
to the old man who stood up
for my son and others
massacred in Tiananmen,
but the thugs watch
my every move.

I am a Tiananmen mother.
It is my duty to weep
for the lost ones.

Harsh Brushstrokes

Acid laden, you paint people
Into little still life scenes
And sour them with sarcasm.
Harsh is your favorite color.
It embellishes most all you touch.
I remember it as what happens
When watercolor water turns
To a shade of lead-rust.

Harsh Brushstrokes first appeared in *Park University Scribe*

PAT BERGE

His Smile

Chestnut leaves yellow
With morning,
Sun-rise spreads delight.
Ah, you are right.
It's the same as the smile
of our six-month old
Peeping over
Your shoulder.

Haiku

Sit with your friend on
Crisp fall afternoons. Write poems.
Ah, what a pleasure!

Small ants creep along
A peony bud hoping
To open the bloom

Ripe, red apples in
A bowl waiting for your lips
To taste their honey

Sometimes in a storm
The rain won't fall from your eyes
It brews in dark clouds

Actively Dying

He wandered through the house
Looking for a place to die
Death just a heel-step behind,
DiBlasi had written.
He sat in a chair,
Here, he thought, I could die here
In this chair so when they find me
The smell might not be so bad.

Smell, I thought as I sat beside
My husband and his mother
She lay death-still in the hospital bed,
Seemingly asleep. Breathing with her
Mouth open, cheek bones high,
Skin Smooth. No wrinkles after morphine
Around the clock of death,
Ticking off the last hours.
Her breathing pace changed.
He and I glance at each other. Reported.
Nurse said, *Apnea, pause in breath.*
She squeezed Mother's feet and knees.
No splotches, she said. *I don't see any…*
She stopped and looked at us.
It's okay, I said. She went on,
I see no signs…
May be several days,
But (she paused again).
She is actively dying.
He touched his Mother's shoulder,
Mom, we have to leave now.
Knowing the sound of his voice
Her eye lids fluttered
She uttered a low-low moan.
We left.
We walked down the hall and
He said, My sister was right.
It is hard to leave her.

A Piece of Your Soul

Sun on snow covers the hill
Melting, freezing
Melting, freezing
Light dancing with tree shadows
Upon its slick, wet surface.
Simple contrast I can watch
For hours from my cocoon
Parked in the driveway.
Up the hill large stones
Like humpbacks
Hold Earth's ridge from yielding.
February waves black limbs
And dried leaves against
Blue sky and white clouds.
From within I'm lulled
By hum of motor, heater, and
Books of poetry,
Donald Hall, B. H. Fairchild, and Debra DiBlasi.
As I read a page from one then the other,
I pick up my pen and begin to write,
It's Amy Bloom's fault.
She wrote:
People are inclined to pour
Themselves a drink…or get a
Pint of ice cream and watch TV
Or pour brandy right over vanilla ice cream
And save some steps…or read
Great fiction which will take you to another place…
But poetry is the thing that will
Take you inside yourself.
It will hand you back a piece of your soul.

Waves

Waves in the ocean
Or at the table
In between or under
Waves overflow the shore
Mount the stones of conflict
Confused words pulled under,
Turned over, tumbled in the tide
Until confusion becomes the wave
As it mounts.
You don't know
When the waves will come.
There is no time table
Like the ocean tides
Where you can
Go down at sunrise, walk
Out for miles to catch
The color orange
As it splits sky and sand

MISSI RASMUSSEN

Sticks and Stones

Five stick people stand
holding hands
Their long stick fingers
sticking out
The only curves:
their perfect circle heads.
They have no clothes.
They have no shame.
This xylophone-shaped
family of sticks.

On the top of the page
scrawled in squiggly letters
not much more impressive
than the kindergartner's
are the teacher's wise words
that people should have hair
on top of their stick heads
And to please color better
because you know better
than to leave the stick people
naked.

This chemo family.
This skinhead family.
This poor family that can't afford
hats.

Their stick brains
as big as their stick heads
as big as their stick hearts
standing in a row,
holding stick hands
this stick family
of smiles.

Good-bye Present

One day
a long time from now
I will wander
with what I hope is nonchalance
into that big, bright store
you love so much,
and I will find the aisle
with the big glass case
and I will kneel down
to the bottom shelf
(because nothing changes here),
and for just a moment,
maybe with my hand on the glass,
I will look into that big glass case
as if I am looking through a window
into a different world,
and I will consider
for just a moment,
or maybe a long time
asking someone to unlock the case
and handing me one of
the little gray boxes-
one of the little gray boxes
that once ended up
in your Christmas stocking
and once in your hand
for no reason.
Maybe I will lift the flap
of the box
and take a little sniff.

Maybe I will squirt
just a little bit
right there in the store
so I can spread it all around.
Or maybe I will just
get up and leave the store
with only what I went in there to get,
leaving my fingerprints on the glass
and the other world
undisturbed.

The Fine Art of Making Breakfast

As the bacon
pops and spatters,
don't let him know
that you've forgiven him.
Let him brush against
your hip
as you both stand at the stove-
your touches completely
incidental.
Nudge the egg whites
with the spatula
to keep them from
becoming one.
Keep everything on
low heat.

Make him do the hash browns
and handle the mean grease.
Make him cut the onion tips,
make him cry.

Always keep him
on one side of you
so that when the toast falls
it will land between you,
butter side up.

The Fine Art of Making Breakfast was awarded the 2007 Nicholas Manchion Endowed English Scholarship Award

While Reading Frankenstein To My 3-Week Old

While reading Frankenstein
to my 3-week old
she looks up at me,
her mouth forming an "o,"
her eyes still not working
in perfect unison,
her eyelids blinking
as if she is trying them on.

My words are soft,
for that is all it takes
to lull her away…
eventually.
Not the story,
or the subject.
She does not know of
its horror.
She does not know of
her own hands.
I could have chosen
anything.
I could have chosen Beowulf.
I could have chosen Macbeth.

While reading Frankenstein
to my 3-week old
she has finally drifted off to sleep.
My little pink monster.
And I will never
sleep the same again.

Archives

Digging through the archives of my life,
I find the pages of me
wadded up and then smoothed out again
Perhaps placed within
a larger edition
and pressed.

The ink is smudged
underneath my eyes
The black that underlines
my years and experiences
of having not yet died.

I find a question mark.
One crooked line with a tiny dot
so large one million atoms
could fit within it
end to end.

And I am one small dot
on one small dot
within this space
as black as ink
that we sometimes call outer
and sometimes but not often
call inner.

There it is. The broken mirror.
Sharp edges entice me.
Observe the signs:
Do Not Touch, Fragile,
Handle With Care.
Pull by the spine and open.

On the First Day Apart from my Newborn

On this first day
apart,
I sleep,
sedated from the incision.
She looks for me
under closed eyelids.
We have never been
apart before.
And we just can't
take it.

Members

Rebecca Stallard earned a Bachelor's degree in English and Communications from Missouri Western University. She currently resides in Kansas City, Missouri. Rebecca works as a screenwriter with James Gang Productions in Los Angeles and has a self-published children's book, *Cari Fry in the Land of Nye*. Rebecca is an award-winning poet, and is currently working on an autobiography of her family and their dealings with hereditary cancer. Rebecca has also written stage plays, one of which is currently under production at a community theatre in Burbank, California.

Brenda Conley is a student of poetry and an avid fan of listening as it is read. As chapter secretary, her association with the Kansas City Chapter of the Missouri State Poetry Society, KC Metropolitan Verse, brings countless hours of pleasure. Her work can be found in *Grist*, *The Scribe*, and *Under the TellingTree, an Anthology of Verse and Voice*. Enjoying poetry, from classic to contemporary, has become a passion, although, her first love is her family. "My life's goal: to be a mother and a grandmother, and I am. I write poems for my family and loved ones. When they listen, that pleases me."

Amy Leigh wrote her first short story at the age of nine and ever since, has wanted to make stories and poetry her life's work. Her work has appeared in numerous literary anthologies and journals. Her inspirations come from too many poets and writers to list. She is currently working on a fiction novel, *Isadora's Moon*.

Don Fessler writes a lifetime of love and marriage, life and death, on homeland and foreign soil. "I try to write poetry from yesterday, today and tomorrow by Muse, maybe…"

Scot Isom says his poetry can be found on the sides of buildings, undersides of desks, and in the lines of other people's poetry (he believes all poetry is his). He received his Bachelor's from Northeast Missouri State in art and art history. They changed the name to Truman State to try to separate the name of the university from his name. He received his Master's in Art History from the University of Missouri, Columbia, because they were tired of him wandering the halls and just wanted him off the campus. The Kansas City chapter of the Missouri Poetry Society accepted him as a member since the rest of the state's chapters wouldn't claim him.

Bernita Pettit enjoys tracing a line of decent of her family history, or reading a selected book with a local book club. Her real pleasure comes in writing about family ties, especially writing about her children. "There's poetry in every moment remembered." She would like to share those moments.

JD Smith earned her B.S. from Kansas University and her M.A.T. from Webster University in St Louis, Missouri. She has always appreciated poetry. One of her earliest childhood pleasures was memorizing a poem. Children have always been an important part of her life. As an elementary school teacher, one of her goals was to instill a love of poetry in her students. Now, with grandchildren of her own, she shares her passion for poetry with them.

Terry Weide is the author of a fantasy novel, *Dream of Power, Dream of Glory,* which won the 2004 Preditors and Editors poll for best sci-fi/fantasy book. His writing has also appeared in *Flash Me, Flashshot, The Verb, The Sword Review, Whispering Spirits, Alien Skin,* and *Dragons, Knights, and Angels* e-zines, on the Dreamquestone.com, OnceWritten.com, and Wilde Times sites, on Whim's Place, in the anthologies *Nancy's Christmas Eve Visitor, Short Attention Span Mysteries,* and *Distant Passages: The Best from Double-Edged Publishing 2005*, and in the print magazines *Moon Reader, Midday Moon,* and *The Writers Post Journal.* He is the author of a chapbook of poetry, *Suburbs of the Mind*, and a digest book of poetry, stories, and essays, *Skipping Across Creation*, both from Snark Publishing. He thanks all those who take the time to read his work.

Michael A. Wells is a native Missouri poet who views poetry as a life experience. He has been anthologized, and his work has appeared in literary journals as well as newspapers and online venues. His work ranges from serious to humorous and everything he writes is accessible to himself, on occasion it may be to others as well.

Pat Berge, Director of WriterHouse, in Kansas City, inspires writers in her classes at Maple Woods Community College and in her TellingTree Writing Workshops. She is co-editor of *Under the TellingTree: An Anthology of Verse and Voice.* Pat also taught at Columbia College Chicago while studying for her Master of Fine Arts in Creative Writing.

Missi Rasmussen is an award-winning poet and writer whose work has appeared in numerous literary journals, anthologies, and online venues. She was educated at Park University in Parkville, Missouri, with emphases in English and Creative Writing. She is the Founder and President of the Kansas City Chapter of the Missouri Poetry Society and one of its state board representatives. She teaches poetry writing workshops in the Kansas City area, where she lives with her son and daughter.

www.ingramcontent.com/pod-product-compliance
Ingram Content Group UK Ltd.
Pitfield, Milton Keynes, MK11 3LW, UK
UKHW041923190726
13854UKWH00003B/1419

9 781430 320807